THE SIx KEYS
OF EUDOXUS

First Edition 16th or 17th Century
Unknown Author

New Edition 2016
Edited by Tarl Warwick

SIX KEYS OF EUDOXUS

COPYRIGHT AND DISCLAIMER

FOREWORD

The author of this particular alchemical work is not known. Much like many Renaissance-era texts ascribed their manufacture to Solomon, Moses, Paracelsus, Agrippa, Hermes, or other major figures within the occult, it ascribes itself to another philosophical and mathematical genius of prior ages- namely, Eudoxus, a great mind of antiquity, whose works are no longer extant and who is only mentioned in second-hand sources from the same time period and after.

Broken down into six keys (essentially, chapters with different content) the work professes the ability to teach the art of natural science, the creation of alkahest and the stone of the philosophers, in a more simplistic and straightforward manner than others, which are alluded to here in these pages. Through trial and error, and the application of study to other alchemical works, the Six Keys of Eudoxus claims that the student of this "art" will be fully capable of not only creating these substances, but projecting (increasing, via multiplication) their mass. The essential concept is that once the metallic seed of gold is subdued and properly prepared, it is able to affect other materials without great effort, transmuting, for example, lead, mercury, regular gold, or dead earth (depending on the manuscript queried) into the same material that the processed, completed stone is created of. Through this practice a large amount, or some say, inexhaustible amount, of elixir can be made, for the treatment of any malady, or, in some accounts, for the material gain of the student.

In truth much of this content is misconstrued lore at its finest- the chemical processes spoken of either in veiled terms or, less often, plainly, in alchemical texts, have modern counterparts- the creation for example of colloidal gold as *aurum potabile* or the oily byproduct of lead when oxidized in certain manners being used as a special red oil or tincture of the philosophers. This specific work, though, claims the capability of inexhaustible projection.

It should be noted that the specific date of manufacture of this text is not known. I have modernized the English used and inferred the date from the form of its content, the other authors it references, and the alchemical terms (black raven, etc) used in its pages, and it is certainly from the Renaissance- whether the 16th or 17th century remains to be seen.

THE SIX KEYS OF EUDOXUS

THE FIRST KEY

The first key is that which opens the dark prisons in which the sulfur is shut up: This is it which knows how to extract the seed out of the body, and which forms the stone of the philosophers by the conjunction of the spirit with the body- of sulfur with mercury.

Hermes has manifestly demonstrated the operation of this first key by these words: In the caverns of the metals there is hidden the stone, which is venerable, bright in color, a mind sublime, and an open sea.

This stone has a bright glittering: it contains a spirit of a sublime original; it is the sea of the wise, in which they angle for their mysterious fish.

But the operations of the three works have a great deal of analogy one to another, and the philosophers do designedly speak in equivocal terms, to the end that those who have not the lynx's eyes may pursue wrong, and be lost in this labyrinth, from whence it is very hard to get out. In effect, when one imagines that they speak of one work, they often treat of another.

Take heed, therefore, not to be deceived here; for it is a truth, that in each work the wise artist ought to dissolve the body with the spirit; he must cut off the raven's head, whiten the black, and vivify the white; yet it is properly in the first operation that the wise artist cuts off the head of the black dragon and of the raven.

Hence, Hermes says: What is born of the crow is the beginning of this art. Consider that it is by separation of the black, foul, and stinking fume of the blackest black that our astral, white, and resplendent stone is formed, which contains in its veins the blood of the pelican. It is at this first purification of the stone, and at this shining whiteness, that the work of the first key is ended.

THE SECOND KEY

The second key dissolves the compound of the stone, and begins the separation of the elements in a philosophical manner: this separation of the elements is not made but by raising up the subtle and pure parts above the thick and terrestrial parts.

He who knows how to sublime the stone philosophically, justly deserves the name of a philosopher, since he knows the fire of the wise, which is the only instrument which can work this sublimation. No philosopher has ever openly revealed this secret fire, and this powerful agent, which works all the wonders of the art: he who shall not understand it, and not know how to distinguish it by the characters whereby it is described, ought to make a stand here, and pray to God to make it clear to him; for the knowledge of this great secret is rather a gift of heaven, than a light acquired by the natural force of reasoning; let him, nevertheless, read the writings of the philosophers; let him meditate; and, above all, let him pray: there is no difficulty which may not in the end be made clear by work, meditation, and prayer.

Without the sublimation of the stone, the conversion of the elements and the extraction of the principles is impossible; and this conversion, which makes water of earth, air of water, and fire of air, is the only way whereby our mercury can be prepared.

Apply yourself then to know this secret fire, which dissolves the stone naturally and without violence, and makes it dissolve into water in the great sea of the wise, by the distillation which is made by the rays of the sun and moon.

It is in this manner that the stone, which, according to Hermes, is the vine of the wise, becomes their wine, which, by the operations of art, produces their rectified water of life, and their most sharp vinegar. The elements of the stone cannot be dissolved but by this nature wholly divine; nor can a perfect dissolution be made of it, but after a proportioned digestion and putrefaction, at which the operation of the second key of the first work is ended.

THE THIRD KEY

The third key comprehends of itself alone a longer train of operations than all the rest together. The philosophers have spoken very little of it, seeing the perfection of our mercury depends thereon; the sincerest even, as Artefius, Trevisan, Flamel, have passed in silence the preparation of our mercury, and there is hardly one found who has not feigned, instead of showing the longest and the most important of the operations of our practice.

With a design to lend you a hand in this part of the way, which you have to go, and where for want of light it is impossible to know the true road, I will enlarge myself more than others have done on this third key; or at least I will follow in an order, that which they have treated so confusedly, that without the inspiration of heaven, or without the help of a faithful friend, one remains undoubtedly in this labyrinth, without being able to find a happy deliverance from thence.

SIX KEYS OF EUDOXUS

I am sure, that you who are the true sons of science, will receive a very great satisfaction in the explaining of these hidden mysteries, which regard the separation and the purification of the principles of our mercury, which is made by a perfect dissolution and glorification of the body, whence it had its nativity, and by the intimate union of the soul with its body, of whom the spirit is the only tie which works this conjunction.

This is the intention, and the essential point of the operations of this key, which terminate at the generation of a new substance infinitely more noble than the first.

After the wise artist has made a spring of living water come out of the stone, and has pressed out the vine of the philosophers, and has made their wine, he ought to take notice that in this homogeneous substance, which appears under the form of water, there are three different substances, and three natural principles of bodies- salt, sulfur and mercury- which are the spirit, the soul, and the body; and though they appear pure and perfectly united together, there still wants much of their being so; for when by distillation we draw the water, which is the soul and the spirit, the body remains in the bottom of the vessel, like a dead, black, and dredged earth, which, nevertheless, is not to be despised; for in our subject there is nothing which is not good.

The philosopher, John Pontanus, protests that the very superfluity of the stone is converted into a true essence, and that he who pretends to separate anything from our subject knows nothing of philosophy; for that all which is therein superfluous, unclean, dredged- in fine, the whole compound, is made perfect by the action of our fire.

This advice opens the eyes of those, who, to make an exact purification of the elements and of the principles, persuade themselves that they must only take the subtle and cast away the heavy. But Hermes says that power of it is not integral until it be turned into earth; neither ought the sons of science to be ignorant that the fire and the sulfur are hidden in the center of the earth, and that they must wash it exactly with its spirit, to extract out of it the fixed salt, which is the blood of our stone. This is the essential mystery of the operation, which is not accomplished till after a convenient digestion and a slow distillation.

You know that nothing is more contrary than fire and water; but yet the wise artist must make peace between the enemies, who radically love each other vehemently.

Cosmopolite told the manner thereof in a few words: All things must therefore being purged make fire and water to be friends, which they will easily do in their earth, which had ascended with them. Be then attentive on this point; moisten oftentimes the earth with its water, and you will obtain what you seek. Must not the body be dissolved by the water, and the earth be penetrated with its humidity, to be made proper for generation? According to philosophers, the spirit is Eve, the body is Adam; they ought to be joined together for the propagation of their species. Hermes says the same in other terms: "For water is the strongest nature which surmounts and excites the fixed nature in the body, that is, rejoices in it."

In effect, these two substances, which are of the same nature but of different genders, ascend insensibly together, leaving but a little feces in the bottom of their vessel; so that the soul, spirit, and body, after an exact purification, appear at last inseparably united under a more noble and more perfect form than it was before, and as different from its first liquid form as the alcohol of wine exactly rectified and actuated with its salt is different from the substance of the wine from whence it has been drawn; this comparison is not only very fitting, but it furthermore gives the sons of science a precise knowledge of the operations of the third key.

Our water is a living spring which comes out of the stone by a natural miracle of our philosophy. The first of all is the water which issues out of this stone. It is Hermes who has pronounced this great truth. He acknowledges, further, that this water is the foundation of our art.

11

The philosophers give it many names; for sometimes they call it wine, sometimes water of life, sometimes vinegar, sometimes oil, according to the different degrees of preparation, or according to the diverse effects which it is capable of producing.

Yet I let you know that it is properly called the vinegar of the wise, and that in the distillation of this divine liquor there happens the same thing as in that of common vinegar; you may hence draw instruction: the water and the phlegm ascend first; the oily substance, in which the efficacy of the water consists, comes the last, etc.

It is therefore necessary to dissolve the body entirely to extract all its humidity which contains the precious ferment, the sulfur, that balm of nature, and wonderful unguent, without which you ought not to hope ever to see in your vessel this blackness so desired by all the philosophers. Reduce then the whole compound into water, and make a perfect union of the volatile with the fixed; it is a precept of Senior's, which deserves attention, that the highest fume should be reduced to the lowest; for the divine water is the thing descending from heaven, the reducer of the soul to its body, which it at length revives.

The balm of life is hid in this unclean feces; you ought to wash them with this celestial water until you have removed away the blackness from them, and then your water shall be animated with this fiery essence, which works all the wonders of our art.

But, further, that you may not be deceived with the terms of the compound, I will tell you that the philosophers have two sorts of compounds. The first is the compound of nature, whereof I have spoken in the first key; for it is nature which makes it in a manner incomprehensible to the artist, who does nothing but lend a hand to nature by the inclusion of external things, by the means of which she brings forth and produces this admirable compound.

The second is the compound of art; it is the wise man who makes it by the secret union of the fixed with the volatile, perfectly conjoined with all prudence, which cannot be acquired but by the lights of a profound philosophy.

The compound of art is not altogether the same in the second as in the third work; yet it is always the artist who makes it. Geber defines it, a mixture of *Argent vive* and sulfur, that is to say, of the volatile and the fixed; which, acting on one another, are volatilized and fixed reciprocally into a perfect fixity. Consider the example of nature; you see that the earth will never produce fruit if it be not penetrated with its humidity, and that the humidity would always remain barren if it were not retained and fixed by the dryness of the earth.

So, in the art, you can have no success if you do not in the first work purify the serpent, born of the slime of the earth; it you do not whiten these foul and black feces, to separate from thence the white sulfur, which is the Sal Ammoniac of the wise, and their chaste Diana, who washes herself in the bath; and all this mystery is but the extraction of the fixed salt of our compound, in which the whole energy of our mercury consists.

The water which ascends by distillation carries up with it a part of this fiery salt, so that the effusion of the water on the body, reiterated many times, impregnates, fattens, and fertilizes our mercury, and makes it fit to be fixed, which is the end of the second work.

One cannot better explain this truth than by Hermes, in these words: "When I saw that the water by degrees did become thicker and harder I did rejoice, for I certainly knew that I should find what I sought for."

It is not without reason that the philosophers give this viscous liquor the name of Pontic Water. Its exuberant ponticity is indeed the true character of its virtue, and the more you shall rectify it, and the more you shall work upon it, the more virtue will it acquire. It has been called the water of life, because it gives life to the metals; but it is properly called the great Lunaria, because of its brightness wherewith it shines.

SIX KEYS OF EUDOXUS

Since I speak only to you, you true scholars of Hermes, I will reveal to you one secret which you will not find entirely in the books of the philosophers. Some of them say, that of the liquor they make two mercuries- the one white and the other red; Flamel has said more particularly, that one must make use of the citrine mercury to make the imbibing of the red; giving notice to the sons of art not to be deceived on this point, as he himself had been, unless the Jew had informed him of the truth.

Others have taught that the white mercury is the bath of the moon, and that the red mercury is the bath of the sun. But there are none who have been willing to show distinctly to the sons of science by what means they may get these two mercuries. If you apprehend me well, you have the point already cleared up to you.

The Lunaria is the white mercury, the most sharp vinegar is the red mercury; but the better to determine these two mercuries, feed them with flesh of their own species- the blood of innocents whose throats are cut; that is to say, the spirits of the bodies are the bath where the sun and moon go to wash themselves.

I have unfolded to you a great mystery, if you reflect well on it; the philosophers who have spoken thereof have passed over this important point very slightly.

Cosmopolite has very wittily mentioned it by an ingenious allegory, speaking of the purification of the mercury: This will be done, says he, if you shall give our old man gold and silver to swallow, that he may consume them, and at length he also dying may be burnt. He makes an end of describing the whole magistery in these terms: Let his ashes be strewed in the water; boil it until it is enough, and you have a medicine to cure the leprosy. You must not be ignorant that our old man is our mercury; this name indeed agrees with him because He is the first matter of all metals. He is their water, as the same author goes on to say, and to which he gives also the name of steel and of the lodestone; adding for a greater confirmation of what I am about to discover to you, that if gold couples with it eleven times it sends forth its seed, and is debilitated almost unto death; but the Chalybes conceives and begets a son more glorious than the father.

Behold a great mystery which I reveal to you without an enigma; this is the secret of the two mercuries which contain the two tinctures. Keep them separately, and do not confound their species, for fear they should beget a monstrous lineage.

I not only speak to you more intelligibly than any philosopher before has done, but I also reveal to you the most essential point in the practice; if you meditate thereon, and apply yourself to understand it well; but above all, if you work according to those lights which I give you, you may obtain what you seek for.

And if you come not to this knowledge by the way which I have pointed out to you, I am very well assured that you will hardly arrive at your design by only reading the philosophers. Therefore despair of nothing- search the source of the liquor of the sages, which contains all that is necessary for the work; it is hidden under the stone- strike upon it with the red of magic fire, and a clear fountain will issue out; then do as I have shown you, prepare the bath of the king with the blood of the innocents, and you will have the animated mercury of the wise, which never loses its virtue, if you keep it in a vessel well closed.

Hermes says, that there is so much sympathy between the purified bodies and the spirits, that they never quit one another when they are united together; because this union resembles that of the soul with the glorified body; after which faith tells us, there shall be no more separation or death; because the spirits desire to be in the cleansed bodies, and having them, they enliven and dwell in them.

By this you may observe the merit of this precious liquor, to which the philosophers have given more than a thousand different names, which is in sum the great *Alkahest*, which radically dissolves the metals- a true permanent water which, after having radically dissolved them, is inseparably united to them, increasing their weight and tincture.

THE FOURTH KEY

The fourth key of the art is the entrance to the second work (and a reiteration in part and development of the foregoing): it is this which reduces our water into earth; there is but this only water in the world, which by a bare boiling can be converted into earth, because the mercury of the wise carries in its center its own sulfur, which coagulates it. The transforming into earth of the spirit is the only operation of this work. Boil them with patience; if you have proceeded well, you will not be a long time without perceiving the marks of this coagulation; and if they appear not in their time, they will never appear; because it is an undoubted sign that you have failed in some essential thing in the former operations; for to corporify the spirit, which is our mercury, you must have well dissolved the body in which the sulfur which coagulates the mercury is enclosed.

But Hermes assumes that our mercurial water shall obtain all the virtues which the philosophers attribute to it if it be turned into earth. An earth admirable is it for fertility-The Land of Promise of the Wise, who, knowing how to make the dew of Heaven fall upon it, cause it to produce fruits of an inestimable price. Cultivate then diligently this precious earth, moisten it often with its own humidity, dry it as often, and you will no less augment its virtue than its weight and its fertility.

THE FIFTH KEY

The fifth key includes the fermentation of the stone with the perfect body, to make thereof the medicine of the third order. I will say nothing in particular of the operation of the third work; except that the perfect body is a necessary leaven of our paste. And that the spirit ought to make the union of the paste with the leaven in the same manner as water moistens meal, and dissolves the leaven to compose a fermented paste fit to make bread. This comparison is very proper; Hermes first made it, saying, that as a paste cannot be fermented without a ferment; so when you shall have sublimed, cleansed and separated the foulness from the feces, and would make the conjunction, put a ferment to them and make the water earth, that the paste may be made a ferment; which repeats the instruction of the whole work, and shows, that just so as the whole lump of the paste becomes leaven, by the action of the ferment which has been added, so all the philosophic confection becomes, by this operation, a leaven proper to ferment a new matter, and to multiply it to infinity. If you observe well how bread is made, you will find the proportions also, which you ought to keep among the matters which compose our philosophical paste. Do not the bakers put more meal than leaven, and more water than the leaven and the meal? The laws of nature are the rules you ought to follow in the practice of our magistery. I have given you, upon the principal point, all the instructions which are necessary for you, so that it would be superfluous to tell you more of it; particularly concerning the last operations, about which the adepts have been less reserved than at the first, which are the foundations of the art.

THE SIXTH KEY

The sixth key teaches the multiplication of the stone, by the reiteration of the same operation, which consists but in opening and shutting, dissolving and coagulating, imbibing and drying; whereby the virtues of the stone are infinitely able to be augmented. As my design has been not to describe entirely the application of the three medicines, but only to instruct you in the more important operations concerning the preparation of mercury, which the philosophers commonly pass over in silence, to hide the mysteries from the profane which are only intended for the wise, I will tarry no longer on this point, and will tell you nothing more of what relates to the projection of the medicine, because the success you expect depends not thereon. I have not given you very full instructions except on the third key, because it contains a long train of operations which, though simple and natural, require a great understanding of the laws of nature, and of the qualities of our matter, as well as a perfect knowledge of chemistry and of the different degrees of heat which are fitting for these operations. I have conducted you by the straight way without any winding; and if you have well minded the road which I have pointed out to you, I am sure that you will go straight to the end without straying. Take this in good part from me, in the design which I had of sparing you a thousand labors and a thousand troubles, which I myself have undergone in this painful journey for want of an assistance such as this is, which I give you from a sincere heart and a tender affection for all the true sons of science. I should much bewail, if, like me, after having known the true matter, you should spend fifteen years entirely in the work, in study and in meditation, without being able to extract out of the stone the precious juice which it encloses in its bosom, for want of knowing the secret fire of the wise, which makes to run out of this plant (dry and withered in appearance) a water which wets not the hands, and which by a magical union of the dry water of the sea of the wise, is dissolved into a viscous water- into a mercurial liquor, which is the beginning, the foundation, and the key of our art: Convert, separate, and purify the elements, as I have taught you, and you will possess the true mercury of the philosophers, which will give you the fixed sulfur and the uiversal medicine. But I give you notice, moreover, that even after you shall be arrived at the knowledge of the secret fire of the wise, yet still you shall not attain your point at your first career. I have erred many years in the way which remains to be gone, to arrive at the mysterious fountain where the king bathes himself, is made young again, and retakes a new life exempt from all sorts of infirmities. Besides this you must know how to purify, to heal, and to animate the royal bath; it is to lend you a hand in this secret way that I have expatiated under the third key, where all those operations are described. I wish with all my heart that the instructions which I have given you may enable you to go directly to the end. But remember, you sons of philosophy, that the knowledge of our magistery comes rather by the inspiration of heaven than from the lights which we can get by ourselves. This truth is acknowledged by all artists; it is for good reason that it is not enough to work; pray daily, read good books, and meditate night and day on the operations of nature, and on what she may be able to do when she is assisted by the help of our art; and by these means you will succeed without doubt in your undertaking.

This is all I have now to say to you. I was not willing to make you such a long discourse as the matter seemed to demand; neither have I told you anything but what is essential to our art; so that if you know the stone which is the only matter of our stone, and if you have the understanding of our fire, which is both secret and natural, you have the keys of the art, and you can calcine our stone; not by the common calcination which is made by the violence of fire, but by a philosophic calcination which is purely natural.

Yet observe this, with the most enlightened philosophers, that there is this difference between the common calcination which is made by the force of fire and the natural calcination; that the first destroys the body and consumes the greatest part of its radical humidity; but the second does not only preserve the humidity of the body in calcining it, but still considerably augments it. Experience will give you knowledge in the practice of this great truth, for you will in effect find that this philosophical calcination, which sublimes and distills the stone in calcining it, much augments its humidity; the reason is that the igneous spirit of the natural fire is corporified in the substances which are analogous to it.

Our stone is an astral fire which sympathizes with the natural fire, and which, as a true salamander receives it nativity, is nourished and grows in the elementary fire, which is geometrically proportioned to it.

FINIS

SIX KEYS OF EUDOXUS

Made in the USA
Monee, IL
20 January 2022

89491438R00015